The Citizen and the
John Birch Society

The Citizen and the John Birch Society

by

LESTER DeKOSTER

Director of the Library and Professor of Speech
Calvin College

WILLIAM B. EERDMANS PUBLISHING COMPANY
GRAND RAPIDS, MICHIGAN

A Reformed Journal Monograph

This material, in slightly different form, first appeared in the pages of the *Reformed Journal*. It is reprinted in this format by permission of the Publisher and Editors of that magazine. The *Reformed Journal* seeks to provide an outlook on current religious and theological matters from a contemporary Calvinist point of view. It is published ten times during the year and is obtainable on a subscription basis at its office at 231 Jefferson, Grand Rapids, Michigan 49502.

The Citizen and the John Birch Society

THE GREEK PHILOSOPHER PLATO TELLS IN ONE OF HIS dialogues how a young man of Athens, named Hippocrates, awakened his friend Socrates one morning before the dawn had come. "Socrates! Socrates! Please rise at once and go with me!"

"Go where?" Socrates wants to know, sleepily.

"To hear the new teacher who came to Athens just last night!" Hippocrates cries. "Please hurry! Hurry!"

Socrates restrains the youth's impatience a little by asking him what he knows about the credentials of this new teacher. Hippocrates only knows the teacher's name, Protagoras, and that he claims to teach great wisdom.

"Now wait a moment," Socrates says. "If you gave your body over to some trainer to make you strong or skillful in some art, wouldn't you first want to know if the trainer knew his business and was a good trainer?"

"Yes, of course . . . ," Hippocrates admits.

"But, then," Socrates continues, "if you would be so careful of your body, why are you so careless of your soul? Knowledge cannot be carried away like packages in a bag from the grocery store. Knowledge is carried in your very soul. And are you, now, going to this teacher, to let him feed your soul, when you have not even examined his right to be your teacher?"

This question stopped Hippocrates, and it ought to stop each of us. Who has the *right*, amidst all the babble of voices we hear nowadays, really to be your *teacher*, and mine? And I mean, specifically, who has the right to be our teacher in the principles of *true Americanism*?

You will agree, I am sure, that right now there are few more important questions than this. Who can teach us what is the *true* Americanism which has over the years

5

made us a great nation, the *true* Americanism to which every good citizen still aspires?

We need teachers of *good* Americanism. All we can get. Now. Always.

But shall we give our souls to *every* teacher who claims to know what good Americanism is?

No, Socrates' warning is as fresh today as the dawn in which he uttered it. *Test your teachers.*

Yes, also test me, for he who writes presumes to teach.

But a test presumes standards by which the test is made. What are they to be? How do we *know* what *true* Americanism is?

We will find the answer and the standards, no doubt, in the men who formed us as a nation. Those who came centuries ago across stormy seas for the sake of liberty. Those who fashioned civilization out of wilderness. Those who caught up the spirit of the times into Declaration and Constitution, and who told us what they were doing. Those who interpreted these documents in words and deeds as the swift decades passed. They all set the standards. The teacher of *true* Americanism must, it would seem very likely, be steeped in their thoughts and deeds. And he must be trying to live after their models.

Now, I would like you to apply with me these ·standards to a new "teacher" of Americanism, one which calls its magazine *American Opinion*. One which calls its reading rooms *American* Opinion Reading Rooms. One which speaks in its fundamental *Blue Book* about the "true Americanist . . ." (p. 138). One which claims to know how to "make America strong and healthy and a true example for all the world again. . ." (*Blue Book,* p. 142; hereafter *B.B.*). I mean, of course, the John Birch Society.

Is this Society a reliable teacher of *true* Americanism?

It *claims* to be. It *means* to be. I do not question the sincerity of its membership. But *is* it? Is it in fact a sound guide to the mind and spirit proclaimed to all the world in the finest of all political documents, our Declaration of Independence? Is the Birch Society a model of Americanism in action, and therefore able from practical experience to teach us how to act as citizens of these United States? Do Birch Society publications breathe the spirit of our Pilgrim Fathers, of the Founding Fathers, of Lincoln, Theodore Roosevelt, and Wilson, to name no others? Do the *Federalist Papers* determine, along with the great decisions of Justice John Marshall, the Birch Society's understanding of the Constitution? Can a Society which declares that "democracy is merely a deceptive phrase, a weapon of demagoguery, and a perennial fraud" (*B.B.,* p. 159) *really teach* us the meaning of Lincoln's immortal description of America as a "government of the people, by the people, and for the people. . ."? For this is what democracy is!

Once more, can a Society which declares that "government is always and inevitably an enemy of individual freedom" (*B.B.,* p. 130) really teach Americans what our Declaration means when it says that "governments are instituted among men" to "secure" our "right" to "life, *liberty,* and the pursuit of happiness"? When the Preamble to our Constitution clearly declares that a *government* is established by this magnificent document to "form a more perfect Union, establish Justice, insure domestic Tranquillity, provide for the common Defence, promote the General Welfare, and secure the blessings of Liberty to ourselves and our posterity. . . ," how can a Society which openly says that "the greatest enemy of man is, and always has been, government" (*B.B.,* p. 138), I say how can such a "teacher" ever tell us what the Constitution means today?

These are questions which the citizen ought to put to this would-be teacher. The questions simply test that teacher's *right* by virtue of competence to instruct his fellow citizens in the meaning of Americanism. Let us now examine the credentials of this new Society in the light of questions such as these.

Is the John Birch Society qualified to teach you and me what true Americanism is?

Let us take the answer, in the Society's own words, from its own documents, largely from the *Blue Book*. And then let each one, as a free citizen, decide if the JBS is the teacher for him.

DEFENDERS OF THE JOHN BIRCH SOCIETY (HEREAFTER JBS) have a cute way of dealing with criticism of the Society. They attack the critic. And this is their argument: (1) the JBS is, they say, the "most effective" anti-Communist force in the U.S. just now; (2) if anyone dares to criticize the JBS, it follows, they say, that (3) he must be a "Comsymp" or worse. The critic is, in a word, either deliberately or stupidly anti-American, either a knave or a fool.

Now, why in fact should Communism fear the JBS? Let us ask the question, not of the sly Communist, nor of the JBS member, but just of the facts.

Everyone knows that Communism digs in under cover of division, discord, suspicion, unrest, mistrust. Communism is a disease of the mind as well as of society. It feeds on every virus which weakens the mutual trust men have in each other and in their government. This is the environment which it tries to create and then to exploit: division, suspicion, fear, uncertainty.

Now, whether you are or are not a member of the JBS, and whether you are or are not sympathetic to the Society's aims and activities, you can hardly blind yourself to the fact that when it comes to sowing suspicion, fear, uncertainty, unrest, and division in America, the JBS is uncommonly successful.

Do you know any other group that has worked so hard to make Americans suspect the Chief Justice of their highest court? And all the while there is a perfectly legal, constitutional way in which this Chief Justice and any other government official can be charged, tried, and impeached *on the evidence*—without creating all this doubt and suspicion. Of course, the Communists want us to doubt our own courts, and suspect each other in the bargain. Do they weep, then, when this job is neatly done for them?

Or consider the Vietnam conflict. Do you know any organization which has been more confused itself, and which tries to spread more confusion among the American people, about our real aims and purposes in Vietnam, than the JBS? Unless it is the left-wing radicals, who want us to lose face and go home. First, the JBS took its Vietnam "line" from its Belmont headquarters in the slogan, also used for the United Nations: "Get US

Out!" But it finally dawned on Belmont that this is exactly what the Communists want. So in 1966 the orders from headquarters were to say: "Win this war in Vietnam—and then get out!" But this, too, is a left-wing line. So in 1967 the JBS published a pamphlet on Vietnam with still another slogan: "Victory, Then Peace!" But all the while the JBS *Bulletin* keeps telling the JBS, and the JBS keeps trying to teach other Americans, that in fact we are in Vietnam to further "the international Communist conspiracy."

Now, fellow citizen, do you really believe that the Communist movement "fears" this kind of confusion? They could not do half as good a job of beclouding American war aims and peace aims in Vietnam as does the JBS.

As part of its series of "continuing projects," the JBS proclaims the so-called "Liberty Amendment," which would deprive the Federal government of the right to tax incomes. You may be sure that the Communists in and out of the U.S. know very well that without the income tax the Federal government would have very little money to spend on anything, especially on the military. Do you think that the Communists *object* to this "Liberty Amendment" and are worried because the JBS supports it so vigorously? If American power becomes too weak to prevent Communist take-over in all of Asia, all of Africa, all of South America, and in the Near East as well, because with JBS help the "Liberty Amendment" gets passed, are the Communists going to shudder before the JBS, or quietly applaud it while only *pretending* to shudder?

In short, the JBS may *claim* that world Communism in general, and U.S. Communists in particular, tremble at the mention of the JBS. But if they do, it might be that it is a little show put on just conspicuously enough to help JBS Project Number One: *Recruitment!* Because every new member added to the Birch Society becomes one more American spreading dissension, division, suspicion, fear, and discord in his own heart and among his fellow citizens. This he does, no doubt in all sincerity, far more effectively than the Communists have ever been able to do. And when this JBS member actually spreads the rumor that, according to the *American Opinion Score Board,* Communist control in the United States approximates 60 to 80 percent, who gets the shock? Not the Communist Party; they only wish it were true. It is the American citizen who gets, or is supposed to get, the alarm; and then follows, as usual, the argument and charge and discord, from which only Moscow can reap the dividends.

With a few more "enemies" like the JBS, Communism wouldn't need any friends!

Surely Communism is not hurt by JBS attacks on fundamental American principles like democracy and the virtues of government. Whether the JBS knows it or not, Communism finds that its mortal enemy in the struggle for the minds and allegiance of men around the world is American *democracy*. This is why no Communist nation ever allows its people freely to choose between Communism and democracy. They all know that the people would choose democracy.

Imagine, then, the Communist's pleasant surprise when he finds the *Blue Book* viciously turning on democracy as "merely a deceptive phrase, a weapon of demagoguery, and a perennial fraud" (p. 159). No Communist would care to say more. It's all right with him when the *Blue Book* speaks of "that footstool of tyrants known as democracy" (footnote no. 14). And Communism doesn't mind, either, when the *Blue Book* says,

> Government is always and inevitably an enemy of individual freedom (p. 130).

The American Declaration of Independence speaks highly of government. You remember the sentence:

> To secure these rights governments are instituted among men, deriving their just powers from the consent of the governed. . . .

Far from being an evil, government *secures, makes certain of, protects* certain "rights." So says our Declaration.

What *rights*? You know that, too: "life, liberty, and the pursuit of happiness."

Just to set it in order, let me quote the sentences:

> We hold these truths to be self-evident: that all men are cre-

ated equal; that they are endowed by their Creator with certain inalienable rights; that among these are Life, Liberty, and the Pursuit of Happiness; that to secure these ends, governments are instituted among men, deriving their just powers from the consent of the governed. . . .

Well, take your choice: the *Blue Book,* which says that government is *always* the enemy of freedom, or the Declaration of Independence, which says that government in fact *secures* it.

The JBS parts company here, not only with the Declaration but also with the Constitution.

Have you read it lately? It was hammered out by men who, as the *Blue Book* admits, "knew a great deal about history and government" (footnote no. 25). The *Blue Book* underestimates our Founding Fathers with such faint praise. The men who met in Philadelphia for four long months in 1787 combined, on the whole, more wisdom, learning, prudence, patience, courage, and self-denial than the world had yet seen in one assembly. They met for only one purpose. It was to find a solid footing for a strong central government. And what they expected such a government to do, they carefully spelled out in the Preamble to the Constitution they drafted:

WE, THE PEOPLE OF THE UNITED STATES, in order to form a more perfect Union, establish Justice, insure domestic Tranquility, provide for the common Defence, promote the general Welfare, and secure the Blessings of Liberty to ourselves and our posterity, do ordain and establish this CONSTITUTION for the United States of America.

Again, government is "to secure the Blessings of Liberty to ourselves and our posterity." This could not have been written by men who took government to be "the ultimate enemy of all freedom."

Where do you stand? On the *Blue Book,* or on the Constitution? Suit yourself, but don't mistake those millions of Americans who stand where their fathers stood, foursquare on the Constitution, for "Comsymps." If you do, you only make yourself look ridiculous. Because the Communist doesn't happen to be interested in "the Blessings of Liberty" which government "secures." And if you attack government as an "evil," it is you and not the Constitution which talks "Comsymp's" language!

11

Is America a *democracy* or a *republic*?

The John Birch Society seems to think that this is a very important question, one to which they know the answer. America, they say, is not and never was meant to be, a *democracy*. What a strange ring this charge has to American ears. Were our teachers always wrong, then, in urging us ever to be thankful that we lived in a democracy? We fought World War I "to make the world safe for democracy," that is, to preserve our own way of life. And we won that war, and did preserve—*what*, if not democracy? We fought World War II against tyranny, because it is the sworn enemy of democracy. And now we fight a "cold war" and a "hot war" against another tyranny, for the same reason, to preserve *democracy* for ourselves and, if possible, to spread its benign influence upon others.

And what now is all this fuss and feathers about America's not really being a democracy at all? Indeed, what is this raucous and blatant noise about democracy being "merely a deceptive phrase, a weapon of demagoguery, and a perennial fraud" (*Blue Book,* p. 159)? Is everybody else out of step, except the JBS? Did brave men fight and die for a "deceptive phrase," or for a real way of life? Did Americans fight a bloody Civil War to forge a "weapon of demagoguery," or to preserve democracy for us all? Did Washington suffer at Valley Forge to promote a "perennial fraud," or to "establish a new nation, conceived in liberty and dedicated to the proposition that all men are created equal"—which is Lincoln's definition of democracy? You had better make up your mind about these alternatives, for we face crucial problems today that only democracy can hope to surmount. Where do *you* stand?

We know where the JBS stands. It sneers at democracy as "probably the worst of all forms of government" (*B.B.,* footnote 25). And it hopes to cover up this sneer by throwing lots of dust into the air about whether or not America is, or ever was, a democracy. America is, the JBS cries, a republic.

Oh, indeed. And what does this prove about whether or not America is, at the same time, a democracy? Let's be clear about this. When the JBS says, with all the flourish of having made an important discovery, that America is, and always was, a republic, what is the Society really trying to do? It is all too evident what the JBS is trying to do: it is trying to hide the fact that the Society is busily engaged in a *two-pronged attack* upon the American way of life: *one,* by questioning the loyalty of our public servants, thus sowing suspicion and enmity and division among us, but without ever taking the truly American road of proof, trial, and either conviction or exoneration. And, *two,* by questioning the validity of our form of government itself.

John Adams, second President of the United States, said that it is easy to grasp the differences between various forms of government. You could, in fact, work them out for yourself. Just ask the question, Who holds the real political power in a country? If the people do, then you have a *democracy.* If a small elite does, then you have an *aristocracy.* If a small coterie of the wealthy do, then you have an *oligarchy.* And if only one rules, you have a *monarchy.* Aristotle made this division long ago.

Now each of these general types of government can take various forms. A monarchy could be headed by a king, or by a dictator; the key is that the *source* of political power is in one man's hands and he rules "from the top down." A democracy can be a *pure,* or *direct,* democracy in which the people act as their own legislature, judiciary, and executive; or a democracy can be *representative,* in which the people choose some of their number to act for them; the *key* is that the source of political power resides in the hands of the people, from "the bottom up."

The crucial question, always, is this: *who* is the *source* of political *power?* In America it is now and always has been "the people."

Federalist Paper No. 49 puts it this way:

> ... the people are the only legitimate fountain of power, and it is from them that the constitutional charter, under which the several branches of government hold their power, is derived" (p. 337).

Federalist Paper No. 46 says this:

> The federal and state governments are in fact but

different agents and trustees of the people; . . . ultimate authority, wherever the derivative may be found, resides in the people alone" (p. 314).

And when the power is in the hands of the people, we have a democracy.

And this is why the United States is now, always has been, and was *expressly intended* by our Founding Fathers to be, a *democracy*.

Why, then, all this noise about our being a republic? Is not this term also used for American government? And does not the pledge of allegiance to our flag say, plainly, "to the republic for which it stands"? Yes, of course it does, because a republic is one form of democracy! The JBS does not care for this fact, and tries to deny it, but its truth is easy to demonstrate. *A republic is one form of democracy.* (Aristotle discussed four others.)

Suppose, in order to make this clear, we think back to the first colonists who sailed for these shores. Like the Pilgrims who came over on the *Mayflower,* for example. On their way across the Atlantic, the Pilgrims wrote and signed "The Mayflower Compact." This brief document (you can find it in an encyclopedia or American history book) says in its quaint style and spelling that its forty-one signatories do

> covenant and combine ourselves together into a civill body politick . . . to enacte, constitute, and frame such just & equall lawes, ordinances, Acts, constitutions, & offices, from time to time, as shall be thought most meete & convenient for the generall good of the Colonie: unto which we promise all due submission and obedience.

And after they landed, this is just what they did. They met together, "from time to time," to enact laws, enforce them, and attend to other public business. This is a form of democracy. The people of the Colony held the political power, and participated directly in all the acts of government. And as other colonists came, they too did the same thing. All over New England sprang up the famous Town Meetin's, where laws were proposed, discussed, and adopted or defeated with every "citizen" right on hand to speak his piece and cast his vote.

There is a name for this *form* of democracy. It is called *pure,* or sometimes *direct,* democracy. It was on this kind of democracy that America cut its political eyeteeth; and good experience it was. It taught Americans that the people can govern themselves, and that democracy works! Not perfectly, indeed, but so successfully that when the break with England came, we told the world in the Declaration of Independence that government derives its *just powers from the consent of the governed*. And we began our Constitution with, "We the People of the United States. . . ."

But by this time there were more than three million colonists, and many of them had for some decades been unable to conduct all their public business by Town Meetin'. The thirteen colonies had become too large for that. Pure democracy can only take in a small area and limited number of citizens. So we had already established the practice of electing representatives to do the work of government for us, all the while keeping the power of election in the hands of the people. This is still democracy, for the people are the source of political authority and power. What shall this form of democracy be called? It is called a republic, or sometimes, representative democracy.

In short, we can learn from our own history as a nation that democracy means simply that the people keep for themselves the reins of political power. If they exercise this power directly, they enjoy a pure democracy; if they exercise this power through elected representatives, they enjoy a republic. *America is a democracy because it is a republic, and a republic because it is a democracy*. Just as simple as that.

The JBS smoke screen turns out to be a play on words, probably designed to obscure as much as possible the real JBS disdain for democracy. Before we proceed to prove this same point from both the *Federalist Papers* and our best dictionaries, let me quote a JBS pamphlet which all too clearly reveals the true JBS attitude toward our American form of government, call it republic or call it democracy. The pamphlet is a reprint from the Society's so-called *American Opinion* magazine, and is entitled "On the Differences Between a Democracy and a Republic." The writer, who is not named, says:

> Except when utilized by very small units, such as a
> tiny Greek city-state or an American township or

village, democracy has never worked satisfactorily as a form of government (reprint, *Am. Opin.,* Jan., 1961, p. 22).

Notice carefully. The writer argues that only pure democracy works satisfactorily. It is nice of any JBS writer to make this much of a concession to democracy, especially after we know, as the writer should have known, that the *Blue Book* derides democracy as "merely a deceptive phrase, a weapon of demagoguery, and a perennial fraud" (p. 159). Could this unknown JBS writer actually be hinting that when it comes, at least, to pure democracy, the *Blue Book* might be wrong in scorning democracy as "probably the worst of all forms of government" (fn. no. 25)?

What is even more interesting about this statement by our nameless JBS writer, the statement namely that only *pure* democracy works satisfactorily, is that this position exactly contradicts the *Federalist Papers,* which the JBS usually pretends to know and admire. Turn with me to *Paper* No. 10, where James Madison is discussing a subject of some interest to us right now, the differences between a democracy and a republic. In its pure form, Madison says, democracy does not, as our JBS writer says it does, work so satisfactorily. No, says Madison, it suffers from one grave defect, the curse of "faction." By faction Madison says he means "a number of citizens" who are "united and actuated by some common impulse of passion, or of interest, adverse to the rights of other citizens, or to the permanent and aggregate interests of the community" (p. 55).

And Madison says:

> From this point of view it may be concluded that a pure democracy, by which I mean a society consisting of a small number of citizens, who assemble and administer the government in person, can admit of no cure for the mischiefs of faction (p. 59).

Well, take your choice. Who is right, James Madison or the JBS theorist? Perhaps, before you make a decision, you would like to ask if Madison has a "cure" for faction, and if so, how this cure agrees with what the JBS writer says, next, about democracy.

Yes, Madison has a cure for faction. His cure is that

other form of democracy we have been discussing, a *republic*. This is how he puts it:

> To secure the public good and private rights against the danger of such a faction, and at the same time to preserve the spirit and form of popular government, is then the great object to which our inquiries are directed. . . . A republic, by which I mean a government in which the scheme of representation takes place, opens a different prospect, and promises the cure for which we are seeking (pp. 59-60).

How can a republic do this? By taking in so much larger a range of territory, and so many more citizens, than a pure democracy can, a *republic* diffuses and disperses selfish groups into harmless minorities. This is possible through "representation," which is Madison's description of democracy in the form of a republic.

Now it just happens that the JBS writer we have been quoting also has some views on government by representatives, which is what Madison calls a republic. Listen, carefully to what he says, in a sentence which follows directly after the one quoted above:

> Especially when the size of the unit becomes such that "pure democracy" is no longer practicable, and it is necessary for the voters to select representatives to make the actual decisions and do the governing for them, does the deterioration into a mobocracy always become rapid and disastrous (reprint, p. 22).

Did you read it? Carefully? And did you, perhaps, go back to reread what Madison said? If so, then you were struck in the face, weren't you, by the grim fact that the form of government which Madison proposes as the "cure" for factions this writer condemns as "deterioration." Still more, what Madison defines as a "republic," this JBS pamphlet, openly sold at the Society's so-called American Opinion Bookstores, calls "mobocracy." That term has a long and unsavory history. From the time of the Greeks to the lips of Adolf Hitler, "mobocracy" has expressed the tyrant's scorn of government by, of, and for the people. And now the JBS uses it to describe that form of government which is our own, which Madison calls a *republic*. Note again: both Madison and the JBS writer use almost exactly the same language: Madison says that he means by a republic, "a government in   **17** which the scheme of representation takes place...," while our JBS-nameless says he means by a government which rapidly *deteriorates* into "mobocracy" one in which "it is necessary for the voters to select representatives...."

Well, where do you take your stand now? With Madison and the *Federalist Papers* and the Founding Fathers whom these *Papers* represent, or with the JBS? You *may,* of course, sccrn democracy as mobocracy, in both its pure and representative forms. This is how much freedom our American democracy allows us. But you cannot get our Founding Fathers, our Declaration and our Constitution, and our great Presidents and patriots to stand with you. Not one of these calls democracy a "fraud," or a republic a "mobocracy."

After all the JBS excitement about it, are we at last to learn from this pamphlet exactly what difference they think there is between *democracy* and *republic*? Why yes, here it is, quoted in full:

> "The rule of laws, not men," is one of the soundest of all the copybook maxims. And it is the essence of the whole difference between a democracy and a republic. Democracy is the rule of men, not bound by laws—or tradition or precedent—whenever mob psychology can be built up by demagogues to support the demagogue's disdain for the restrictions of law. A republic is rule subject to laws—and tradition and precedent—which laws cannot be changed except by due and deliberate process according to their own provisions (reprint, p. 22).

Clear enough. The writer wants to define democracy as the "rule of men" and republic as "rule subject to laws." If this is, as the writer blandly and cumbersomely says, "the essence of the whole difference between" them, then of course Madison must have seen that, too. For I judge that Madison may be taken as an authority at least as good as our JBS scribe. So let us ask, before examining for ourselves this matter of "men" versus "law," what Madison has to say. Turn once more to *Federalist* No. 10:

> The two great points of difference between a democracy and a republic are: first, the delegation of the government, in the latter, to a small number of citizens elected by the rest; secondly, the greater number of

citizens, and greater sphere of country, over which the latter may be extended (p. 60).

But, not a syllable about the neat little JBS distinction between "law" and "men." And yet Madison is here pointing out *the* two "great points of difference," which certainly means what our JBS writer calls the "essence of the whole difference. . . ." Madison returns to the distinction in *Paper* No. 14. Let us heed what he says there:

> The true distinction between these forms was also adverted to on a former occasion. It is, that in a democracy, the people meet and exercise the government in person; in a republic, they assemble and administer it by their representatives and agents. A democracy, consequently, will be confined to a small spot. A republic may be extended over a large region (p. 83).

Once more, a loud silence over what the JBS calls the "essence of the whole difference," namely "men" or "law." And yet, again, Madison speaks of *the* "true distinction" between democracy and republic.

For a last lesson from the *Federalist,* on this subject, let us turn to *Paper* No. 39, where Madison is once more defining his terms, this time just a republic:

> If we resort for a criterion to the different principles on which different forms of government are established, we may define a republic to be, or at least may bestow that name on, a government which derives all its powers directly or indirectly from the great body of the people, and is administered by persons holding their offices during pleasure, for a limited period, or during good behavior. It is *essential* to such a government that it be derived from the great body of society, not from an inconsiderable proportion, or a favored class of it (p. 251).

It is very obvious that James Madison, frequently acclaimed to this day as one of the ablest students of government among our Founding Fathers, does *not* view "law" as the "essential" characteristic of a republic. It is equally obvious, from our previous quotations, that Madison does *not* consider government "by men" as opposed to government "by law" as constituting the "true difference" between a republic and a democracy. Wherever our JBS writer got his definition of this difference, he did *not* get it from Madison. Nor did he get it, as we shall shortly observe, from the dictionary. And he is unable to quote in his support from any Founding Father or leading American statesman. It would be useful to know if, perhaps, he made up his distinction by himself. In any case, Americans looking for teachers about their form of government would do well to stick to James Madison.

Yet this JBS writer brazenly tries to leave the impression that Madison supports him, though he is careful not to quote from him. Listen to this, from the same JBS pamphlet we have been using:

> And one of the very few times the Federalist Papers (which tell us most of what we know about the thinking that went into our constitution) even mention democracy, is in Federalist Paper No. 10, where Madison does so in order *to show us its disadvantages* (reprint, p. 22; italics his).

It is amusing how JBS writers try to make something against democracy out of the fact that the term is not heavily used by early writers and documents; because, of course, every time the Founding Fathers use "republic" they *mean* one *form* of democracy, that is, sovereignty in the hands of the people. It is like complaining of a painter that he keeps using the words "blue" and "green" but he never mentions the word "color." But he does, of course, every time he says "blue." And so did our forefathers mention "democracy" every time they said "republic." They simply meant, as Madison clearly says once and again, a democracy made representative and encompassing wider territory and more people.

If, now, you will look closely at the last sentence I have quoted from the JBS pamphlet, you can learn a little about the practice of deceit. For this sentence is quite deliberately calculated to mislead. Let me number the tricks in this one sentence—assuming of course that the writer has really studied *Paper* No. 10. If not, he has no business pretending to know what it says.

(1) Madison speaks of *one* disadvantage in *Federalist* No. 10. We already know what it is: "faction." The JBS writer speaks of "disadvantages" as if there were many. Cheap trick.

(2) Madison attributes the disadvantage of "faction"

to *one* form of democracy, and *carefully says this* (check back to our quotation above, or look at *Federalist* No. 10 for yourself); he is discussing "pure" democracy. The JBS writer carefully omits "pure" and wants us to believe that Madison is critical of democracy *as such*. It is true that at the end of *Paper* No. 10 Madison uses "democracy" without the adjective "pure" but by then he knows that we know what he means—at least if we want to be honest about it.

(3) Madison mentions democracy in *Federalist* No. 10 in order to compare its *pure* form with its form as a *republic*, to show that the representative democracy of a republic offers a cure for "faction." The JBS writer wants to leave the impression that Madison alludes to democracy only to show us its disadvantages, and no more. Another effort to mislead.

(4) Madison, as we have already seen, carefully and explicitly states "the two great points of difference between a democracy and republic." This is exactly the object of the JBS pamphlet which, you remember, has for its very title, "On the Difference Between a Democracy and a Republic." What Madison says, as we have noticed, does not at all agree with what the JBS writer is trying to sell us. So the JBS writer *carefully avoids* even mentioning Madison's dealing with his subject, even though he brazenly refers to *Paper* No. 10.

(5) What the JBS writer wishes to do is leave the impression that *Federalist* No. 10 is on his side and supports his view. What he hopes we will not find out is that he perverts Madison's purpose, ignores his main point, and misrepresents what he has to say.

Let's at least be candid and admit that our JBS writer gets a lot of deception into one sentence. But when he says that the *Federalist Papers* "tell us most of what we know about the thinking that went into our constitution," we naturally wonder why, if so, he doesn't care to *listen* to what the *Papers* say. Isn't the thinking that went into our constitution good enough for the JBS? Does the JBS have to invent its own definition of democracy and of republic? Why? To cover up its scurrilous attacks upon the democratic way of life?

Yes, I say "invent its own definition" of the difference between democracy and republic, because the true source book for definitions, the dictionary, only supports Madison's interpretation that democracy can be either pure or representative, that is, either direct democracy or democracy in the form of a republic. Let's just sample the best of the American dictionaries, starting with *Webster's Seventh New Collegiate Dictionary* of 1963:

> Democracy: government by the people; especially rule of the majority. A government in which the supreme power is vested in the people and exercised by them directly or indirectly through a system of representation usually involving periodically held free elections.

Merriam-Webster's *New International Dictionary of the English Language,* third edition, 1963, widely regarded as the best:

> Democracy: a form of government in which the supreme power is vested in the people, and exercised by them directly or indirectly through a system of representation; called also representative democracy.

Try a specialized kind of dictionary, like *Black's Law Dictionary,* fourth edition, 1951:

> Democracy: that form of government in which the sovereign power resides in and is exercised by the whole body of free citizens, as distinguished from a monarchy, aristocracy, or oligarchy. According to the theory of pure democracy, every citizen should participate directly in the business of governing, and the legislative assembly should comprise the whole people. But the ultimate lodgment of the sovereignty being the distinguishing feature, the introduction of the representative system does not remove a government from this type.

And lest anyone contend that all these dictionaries have been influenced by the "deterioration" introduced among us through the New Deal and its offspring, let's take two published before the New Deal got under way: the famous *New Century Dictionary,* edition of 1927:

> Democracy: government by the people; a form of government in which the supreme power is vested in the people and exercised by them or their elected agents.

Or the *Webster's Collegiate,* fourth edition, 1933:

> Democracy: government by the people; government in which the supreme power is retained by the people and exercised by representation, as in a republic.

When words are in dispute, the best authority to settle the argument is the dictionary. That is what dictionaries are for. They see to it, if we heed them, that all of us use the same term in about the same way. If each of us goes off on his own, using terms as he likes, only confusion can result. This is what the JBS is trying to do with the terms *democracy* and *republic*. I wonder why the JBS wants to create confusion among Americans?

But if our republic *is in fact democracy,* as the dictionaries imply, then the *Blue Book* is talking right at our form of government, right now, as the "worst" and as "fraud" and so on.

And is this the Society which presumes to teach good Americans how to be better *Americans*?

In a reprinting of the *Blue Book,* Mr. Welch adds a lame and smirking footnote about the public revulsion occasioned by the *Blue Book* slander of democracy. He says, "Our Liberal critics would have you believe that this statement, for an American, is practically a heresy ..." (footnote no. 25) He means his statement that democracy is "merely a deceptive phrase . . . ," etc.

On the contrary, sir! Wrong as usual. It is not just the "Liberal critics" who are shocked by this grotesque assertion of yours. It is every good American, liberal and conservative alike. And you know it! Moreover, Americans do not view your remarks as *practically* "heresy." Americans, who are sensitive to slurs upon their way of life, take your slander as far worse than "heresy"; they think of it what Mr. Buckley said about your *American Opinion,* as "paranoid and unpatriotic drivel"! (See *National Review,* Oct. 19, 1965, p. 917.)

But to escape this host of authorities, the JBS tries to palm off on the American people its own definitions of republic, as "rule of law," and democracy, as "rule of men." We have observed the hanky-panky an anonymous JBS writer tries to play with *Federalist Paper* No. 10 to lend fictitious support to this invention of definitions. And we will briefly, in a moment, analyze Mr. Welch's equally flimsy attempt to get away with the same deception.

Meanwhile, fellow Americans, rejoice that democracy is big enough, and strong enough, and free enough, in this great republic of ours, even to shelter a Society which tries so hard to undermine it. For if *democracy* is called a "fraud," this is also an attack on *republic*. And if representative democracy is charged with rapidly deteriorating into "mobocracy," this is an open slander of our republic. And now, by the way, we can understand why the JBS so freely and carelessly questions the loyalty of those officials elected by the people to administer democracy for us; the JBS simply has no use for democracy.

Does anyone still doubt it? Let us number a few contrasts between the JBS and democracy:

(1) American democracy rests upon our Constitution. As George Washington said in his famous "Farewell Address," which the JBS might read occasionally: "The basis of our political systems is the right of the people to make and alter their constitutions of government." The JBS does not recognize, for itself, this right. It has no constitution.

(2) Our Constitution was, as Washington also said in the same Address, our "own choice." It was adopted only after long discussion, by vote. The JBS has never adopted any program by vote.

(3) Our Constitution protects liberty by providing for the *election* of representatives of the people. The JBS officials are appointed from "the top." Take a look some time at the JBS *Bulletin* for December, 1967, pages 4 to 14. Four "very worthy additions" to the JBS Council are there being "announced" to the membership of the Society. No nomination. No discussion. No election. Just an announcement! Meet the new boss, Joe! (If you don't like this, you are of course always "free"—to get out!) And this is the Society which pretends to teach us good Americanism?

(4) Our Constitution provides that elected officials stand for regular reelection against anyone who wants to run against them. This is because our forefathers were absolutely convinced that periodic election is the only democratic safeguard against tyranny. In the JBS no official has ever stood for election in the first place; so,

of course, none has to submit himself to reelection, either. Nice, if you can get away with it; but hardly in the American pattern.

(5) Our Constitution provides legal ways of removing from office those officials who deserve, in the people's judgment, such removal. The JBS has no such protection. And so all of the suggestions from friends of the JBS, as *National Review* once was, that it is past time for Mr. Welch's retirement flow like water off the duck's back.

(6) Our Constitution carefully provides for a separation of powers, legislative, executive, judicial. The JBS only knows "smoothly functioning direction from the top" (*B.B.*, p. 159). Correction: not always, it appears, quite so "smoothly functioning," but still "from the top."

(7) Our Constitution, and the parliamentary procedures operative under it, protect through judicial process the rights of the minority against the majority. The JBS recognizes one right for the minority, as follows: "Those members who cease to feel the necessary degree of loyalty can either resign or will be put out before they can build up any splintering following of their own inside the Society" (*BB.*, p. 161). If American democracy treated the Birch Society in this way, where would the JBS go?

In fact, fellow American, if you want to know what our democratic republic really means to you, just meditate for a while on what life in this country would be like if the JBS pattern were in control. What if we all were subject to control "from the top down" instead of being, as we are, ourselves in control "from the people up"? Do you recall where, around the world, control from the top is now in effect?

There is no real and essential contradiction between a democracy and a republic. The one is a form of the other. But there is a real and fundamental and absolute contradiction between government "from the top" and government "from the people." We Americans fought a revolutionary war over *this* difference, and have fought wars ever since to make that difference stick.

Isn't it surprising, indeed isn't it amazing, that any

red-blooded, freedom-loving, independent, and self-sufficient American would for one minute sacrifice his hard-won liberty of choice to "direct authority at every turn" (*B.B.*, p. 161)? Come on, fellow citizen. Shake it off. Sing *Yankee Doodle* a few times as our forefathers sang it. And get your shoulder to the wheel of that democratic republic they fashioned for us. *It needs us all.* Right now!

"PRACTICE WHAT YOU PREACH." THE WISDOM SUMMED up in these four words comes to expression in all kinds of maxims like these: *what you are speaks so loudly, I can't hear what you say;* or, *don't tell me, show me;* or, *the proof of the pudding is in the eating;* or, *handsome is as handsome does.* You could name many more old adages, all amounting to the same truth, namely that *practice is the ultimate test of sincerity.*

This means that a Society that presumes to teach Americans how to be good "Americanists" ought itself to be a model of Americanism. Let it have a model constitution, carefully discussed and finally adopted by vote of the founding membership. Let its candidates for office be nominated, heard, and judged on their merits, and elected by secret ballot. Let officers serve for limited terms, subject to reelection, and under control of the constitution. This is, beyond dispute, the *American* model. And Americans say quite simply to any Society that attempts to tell them what *American* opinion ought to be: *practice what you preach.*

We would do some injustice to the JBS if we supposed that they have no answer for this question. But it turns out to be the same tired old answer which advocates of the un-American model have always used: *this is an emergency!* Shades of every dictator and would-be dictator from the beginning of time: *this* is an emergency! And the greater the emergency, the better! The *Blue Book* is surprisingly frank about this old technique:

> Another thing we should do, and one badly needed, would be to start shocking the American people ... (p. 94).

And the form of the "shock" is always the same: an "enemy" is about to take over. Therefore, set aside democracy for "the immediate future" until the emergency is over. There isn't time now for democratic procedures. The scenes change over the centuries, but the excuse is always the same. So "start shocking the American people," and perhaps they will not notice that the JBS is run on an un-American model. Listen to the shock treatment which the *Blue Book* itself attempts:

> For the truth I bring you is simple, incontrovertible, and deadly. It is that, unless we can reverse forces which now seem inexorable in their movement, you have only a few more years before the country in which you live will become four separate provinces in a world-wide Communist dominion ruled by police-state methods from the Kremlin (p. 9).

The shock pattern was clearly set. And the JBS loyally carries on that pattern to this very hour with endlessly dire predictions on the same theme: "The Communists are winning! Watch out! They are creeping in the windows and sneaking in the doors!" To keep the American people as alarmed as possible about the Communists' progress, the JBS has devised a "Scoreboard," which annually gives the Communists more and more "control" of the USA. In 1960, for example, the "score" was about "forty percent" Communist "control" of the USA; last year, 1967, the "score" had leaped to "from sixty to eighty percent control." What, do you suppose, will that "Scoreboard" be using for the shock treatment if it should last another five years? or ten?

The point for Americans to catch is that all this is supposed to cover up the fact that the JBS is run on a completely un-American principle, namely from the top down instead of from the membership up. Or, if we do catch on that the JBS model is not the American pattern, the shock treatment is supposed to persuade us that the emergency is so great, and growing so fast, that there is no time for democratic procedures.

But "shock treatment" is not in the American tradition either. George Washington faced emergencies, one after another for seven long years of the Revolutionary War, but he never descended to the level of trying to shock his fellow citizens into letting him take over and run America from the top. Washington kept no public "Scoreboard" of how well the British were doing. Especially not as a device for shocking the American people into deserting democratic procedures for the time of the emergency. Nor did Lincoln play this kind of game. The shock treatment as an excuse for bypassing democracy does not have an American pedigree. If you want to find a recent example of its use, start with Hitler's *Mein Kampf,* and consider thoughts like:

> All propaganda has to be popular and has to adapt its spiritual level to the perception of the least intelligent of those toward whom it intends to direct itself. . . . All effective propaganda has to limit itself only to a very few points and to use them like slogans until even the very last man is able to imagine what is intended by such a word. . . . Propaganda has to confine itself to little and to repeat this eternally (*Mein Kampf,* pp. 232, 234, 238).

The shock treatment is propaganda. It is intended to justify such suggestions as these, taken from the *Blue Book*:

> What is not only needed, but is absolutely imperative, is for some hardboiled, dictatorial, and dynamic boss to come along . . . (p. 117).

> But the confusion and the problem will get steadily worse; and the need for somebody who can simply say "Help this guy, or let him help you, but stay away from that one" is also going to increase (p. 161).

> I want to convince you, as I am convinced, that only dynamic *personal* leadership offers any chance for us to save either our material or our spiritual inheritance (p. 123).

The shock treatment is not, first of all, interested in the facts. It is first of all interested in scaring people, hoping that if they are scared enough, they will lose faith in themselves, and in their democratic way of life, and turn to a "boss" who alone offers them a "chance" to save their material and spiritual inheritance, no doubt in that order.

And this is why the shock treatment has always to be stepped up. If a score of forty percent Communist "control" does not bring in enough frightened JBS members, then try sixty to eighty percent. And if that still does not produce the "one million members" the *Blue Book* hoped for ("We are out to get a million members truly dedicated to the things in which we believe," p. 165), why, let's also try insinuating that public officials are disloyal, that the Chief Justice ought to be impeached, and that "the Negro revolution" is controlled by Communists. *Let's try anything* . . . so long as it might give the shock treatment.

Once you catch on to this technique, you can read the JBS efforts to step up the "treatment" in every new charge and insinuation the Society makes. You know that the "score" is going to go up. You know that the predictions of imminent disaster are going to become more shrill, until even *National Review* has to call them "drivel."

And if you can get in a word edgewise, amidst all the shouting and confusion, the sober American will simply and quietly remind the JBS that the American way to face an emergency has always been to turn so much more confidently, not to a "boss," but *to the people.* Consider the words of James Madison, spoken long ago in *Federalist Paper* No. 46, and just as true today. Madison, you remember, lived in emergency times all right, but he didn't try the shock treatment. He said,

> These gentlemen must here be reminded of their error. They must be told that the ultimate authority, wherever the derivative may be found, resides in the people alone. . . .

For Madison, the greater the emergency the more it pointed to *the* American model: *the people.* This is where, for every great American, emergency has always pointed: back to the people.

If there is any plain lesson to be learned from the Greeks and the Romans, from Spain and Italy and Germany, from Hitler and Mussolini and Julius Caesar, it is that "emergency" is just an excuse for rejecting democracy and democratic procedures by those who do not believe in democracy in the first place. But if we have any plain lesson to learn from our Founding Fathers, from the Revolution and the Civil War, from our greatest Presidents and patriots, it is that "emergency" *never* furnishes an excuse for turning to an undemocratic model; it always points us once more back to *the people.*

And that is why more and more Americans see through the JBS shock treatment, and the Society has to run its phony Scoreboard higher and higher to try and get results. Says the *Blue Book*:

> The Cold War in which we are engaged is certainly no
> game. It is a fatal struggle for freedom against slavery,
> for existence against destruction (p. 10).

How very true! And in this struggle, the *American*
method is to save freedom by vigorous practice of democracy, for one and for all. Not by submission to "completely authoritative control at all levels" (*B.B.*, p. 159).

Says the *Blue Book,*

> But this is no cream-puff war we are in, and the stakes
> involved are not those of a pillow fight (p. 103).

Well, well. Was it a "cream-puff war" we were in
against the British? George Washington needed no scoreboard to tell him how much control the enemy had over
the colonies. There were those, not a few, who thought
in 1777-78 that soon British control might be exactly
100%. American troops were unpaid, underequipped, in
rags and hungry. Washington was urged that this "emergency" called for action from the top. Why didn't he
take the Army, subdue the Continental Congress, which
was "wasting its time in democratic procedures" while
failing to raise money and munitions of war, and set
himself up as "king"? Washington's response was brief
and pointed: Banish such thoughts from your minds, he
said, and never let me hear one syllable of them again.
Emergency is no excuse for turning against democracy.

His advice is still valid. When you hear talk that the
"emergency" requires an un-American way to meet it,
banish the thought from your mind.

The Civil War was no "cream-puff" war either. Did
Lincoln use the excuse of grave emergency to assume
authority from the top down? No, he ran for his second
term of office while the war was raging; and the election
campaign was no "pillow fight" either. If the *Blue Book*
had been at Gettysburg would it have asked for a' reded-
ication to "government of the people, by the people, and
for the people"?

No, we know what the *Blue Book* thinks of government; it calls it "the greatest enemy of man ..." (p.
138). And we know what it thinks of government of, by,
and for the people; for it calls democracy "merely a
deceptive phrase, a weapon of demagoguery, and a perennial fraud" (p. 159). If, therefore, the *Blue Book* had

been at Gettysburg, it would no doubt have asked for "far more work and dedication, and far more sacrifice of other interests . . . than you ever thought of giving to any other organization . . ." (*B.B.*, p. 166), but *not* to the national government of the United States, *not* to the American way of life, but to a Society. To the JBS, which trusts its own membership so little that its leadership wishes

> to keep strict and careful control on what every chapter is doing, and even every member of every chapter so far as the effective work of the John Birch Society is concerned (*B.B.*, p. 165).

Whatever model such a Society is framed on, one thing is sure: it is not the American model.

Without pointing to other examples from American history, which the reader can easily do for himself, let the conclusion be carefully spelled out. In an emergency, you can choose one of two ways: (1) the JBS way of turning to organization controlled from the top; or, (2) the American way of turning to the people. This latter was Daniel Webster's way, as the clouds of the coming Civil War lowered over the land; *never forget,* Webster thundered, that

> ours is the people's government, made for the people, made by the people, and answerable to the people.

And Theodore Parker, speaking in 1850:

> A democracy is a government of all the people, by all the people, and for all the people.

These noble expressions, by these noble Americans, do not appear in the *Blue Book* of the John Birch Society.

Naturally, the JBS uses the "emergency" excuse also to bypass the democratic procedures of *parliamentary law*. When government is in the hands of the people, and law is made by their representatives, there must be a system of rules under which the legislature operates. This system is called *parliamentary law,* after the English Parliament where it was first introduced. We also call it "Rules of Order." The commonest and best compilation of those rules is that made by Henry M. Robert, and called *Robert's Rules of Order.* Webster said that he kept the handbook of parliamentary law next to his

Bible. Think for a moment what it means to live in a democracy where laws are made according to *rules of order,* instead of living in the kind of country where laws are handed down from the top. Then you will know what Webster meant.

Then you will appreciate, too, what *Robert's Rules* means by saying, in its opening statement of "Principles":

> American Parliamentary Law is built upon the principle that rights must be respected: rights of the majority, of the minority, of individuals, of absentees, and rights of all of these together (75th Anniver. Edn., p. 5).

If this is what parliamentary law implies, then what does the *Blue Book* mean by saying:

> There are many reasons why, in the fight immediately ahead, we cannot stop for parliamentary procedures or a lot of arguments among ourselves (p. 160).

Reread the sentence again. The JBS "cannot stop for parliamentary procedures," that is, it cannot stop for "the principle that rights must be respected ..." within the organization. Why not? The same old argument: this is a fight, and an emergency excuses undemocratic procedures. If our Founding Fathers had believed this, they would never have taken four months to form, through parliamentary debate, the Constitution. They would never have taken another year of popular debate to get it adopted.

But our Founding Fathers believed, and risked their lives for believing, that, as Robert puts it,

> *Rules of Order* is based upon the same enduring principles on which our nation itself is founded—the right of the majority to decide, the right of the minority to be heard, the right of the absentees to be protected (p. 13).

Not so, the *Blue Book*. Hear what it has to say on this vital matter:

> Actually, we are going to cut through the red tape and parliamentary briar patches and road blocks of confused purpose with direct authority at every turn (p. 161).

As usual, the *Blue Book* cannot quite hide the sneer. What Webster valued enough to place next to his Bible, the JBS brushes aside as "parliamentary briar patches."

Well, what about you, fellow American? Do you stand with the American tradition of parliamentary rules of order? Or with the JBS?

Robert goes on to say this:

> In ordinary deliberative assemblies, the right to debate questions before taking final action upon them should never be suppressed by less than a two-thirds vote ... (p. 16).

Not so in the John Birch Society.

> We are not going to have factions developing on the two-sides-to-every-question theme (*B.B.*, p. 161).

We know. For the JBS there is only *one* side to every question; the JBS side. And within the Society, although "we can allow for differences of opinion" and "we shall need and welcome advice," yet "whenever differences of opinion become translated into a lack of loyal support, we shall have short cuts for eliminating both without going through any congress of so-called democratic processes" (*B.B.*, pp. 161-62).

The sneer again: "so-called democratic processes."

And is this the Society which actually presumes to teach us good Americanism?

"We are not a copy of any movement of the past," says the *Blue Book* proudly (p. 169). How true! Least of all a copy of the American past. Nor of the American present. Nor, let us trust, of the American future.

"We are unique," boasts the *Blue Book* (p. 169).

Oh, no! Not *unique* at all. Any of us can, without half trying, think of groups and parties and societies who sneer at democracy, scoff at parliamentary "briar-patches," reject "so-called democratic processes," and operate "under direct authority at every turn." Such groups are not "unique" in this world. They surround us. But why should Americans copy them instead of modeling themselves upon our own forefathers?

The *Blue Book* says that "there are many reasons why, in the fight immediately ahead, we cannot stop for parliamentary procedures. . . ." Take a look sometime at pages 160-161 to find these "many reasons." You will find just *one*. It is the argument that there is "increasing confusion, cleverly planned by the Communists, as to what persons, books, activities and organizations really

33

are anti-Communist" (p. 160). And to cut through all of this planned "confusion," as well as to keep it from infiltrating the JBS, there will have to be "direct authority at every turn."

Sound familiar? Yes, it's the same old argument: this is an emergency. And so there is no time for debate and discussion. Moreover, there is the same old implied insult: you Americans, even those who join the JBS, simply aren't with it when it comes to fighting Communism. You need a "boss" to direct you. Read the *Blue Book,* page 160:

> Now there are ways of sizing up both individuals and organizations in this battle, which come only with experience, a knowledge of the interlocking pieces and personalities, and a feel for the way the Communists work.

And who, then, has this essential experience? Yes, you guessed it. The writer of the *Blue Book,* and head of the JBS, Mr. Robert Welch. He modestly sets himself apart from ordinary Americans, saying ". . . I have a fairly sensitive and accurate nose in this area" (*B.B.,* p. 161).

Trusting the sensitivity, and the accuracy, of Mr. Welch's nose, the JBS wants to "cut through the red tape and parliamentary briar patches and road blocks of confused purpose with direct authority at every turn" (*B.B.,* p. 161). Do *you* want to bet, even for the emergency, what Robert calls "the same enduring principles on which our nation is founded" on the accuracy of one man's nose? If you do, go ahead. But don't call that vast majority of us who prefer parliamentary rights "Comsymps," unless you want to look doubly ridiculous. Especially since *National Review* published on October 19, 1965, its "scoreboard" on just how reliable Mr. Welch's "nose" has turned out to be. In the fight against Communism, said the *Review,* we *cannot even say* that "the John Birch Society is better than nothing. It is—for reasons shown—worse than nothing" (p. 927).

And if you have been wondering why *Robert's Rules of Order* holds such high rank among Americans, it is because *Robert's Rules* is derived from the parliamentary principles set down for the American Congress by Thomas Jefferson himself, between 1797 and 1801. You may not find Jefferson's *Manual,* as it is called, in any

American Opinion Library—the JBS doesn't have any use for it. But your Congressman will probably send you a copy on request. You will notice that Jefferson says in his Introduction,

> These forms, as instituted by our ancestors, operated as a check and control on the actions of the majority, and they were, in many instances, a shelter and protection to the minority against the attempts of power (p. 116).

A good thing to remember the next time someone tries to sell you on the notion that we haven't time, in this emergency, for "parliamentary briar patches" or for "a lot of arguments among ourselves" (*B.B.,* p. 160).

There was *no* excuse, Washington and Jefferson and the others believed, that could ever justify cutting through the so-called parliamentary "briar patches" with direct action. No excuse, *then*; no excuse, *ever*! Why not? Because this cutting through, this direct action, this authority at every turn, all this is what tyranny is! And the Founding Fathers had all they wanted of tyranny. They feared it. They hated it. They fought with their very lives against it. And they chose democracy, with all its delays, all its talk on every side of every question, as the most precious political possession of man. They forged that democracy for themselves and their posterity. And we Americans mean to keep it!

Which reminds us once more of the familiar JBS argument that America is not, and was not meant to be, a democracy at all, but a republic. We have already seen that this argument is false, according to the *Federalist Papers* and according to the dictionaries, all of which show republic to be *one* of the forms of democracy. Why, then, bother now with Mr. Welch's lame attempt to repeat the JBS line once more, in his pamphlet *Republics and Democracies?*

Briefly, for three reasons: (1) to illustrate once more the way JBS writers, from the top down, use quotation; (2) to look at the contention of the JBS that "Greece and Rome" warn us against democracy; and (3) to examine the argument used by the JBS that a republic is government "by law," while a democracy is government "by men."

Speaking of the terms *democracy* and *republic,* this is what Mr. Welch's pamphlet says:

> Also, by the time of the American Revolution and Constitution, the meanings of the words "republic" and "democracy" had been well established and were readily understood.
>
> The two words are not, as most of today's Liberals would have you believe—and as most of them probably believe themselves—*parallels* in etymology, or history, or meaning. The word Democracy (in a political rather than a social sense, of course) had always referred to a type of government, as distinguished from monarchy, or autocracy, or oligarchy, or principate. The word Republic, before 1789, had designated the quality or nature of a government, rather than its structure
>
> (*Republics and Democracies,* p. 17).

Mr. Welch confidently says that "the two words are not . . . *parallels* in etymology. . . ." Etymology is the science of word histories. Inasmuch as the chief authority in etymology is the dictionary, and inasmuch as the dictionary does say precisely that democracy and republic *are* parallel terms, we find Mr. Welch here, as so often when he makes a pretense at scholarship, talking through his hat.

For another example of the same fumbling attempt to deception, look at his argument that "history" proves that *republic* is not *democracy.* He pretends here to quote from the celebrated American historian, Will Durant. You will find Dr. Durant's name dropped on pages 11, 13, 15, 16, and 18 of the pamphlet we are discussing. No doubt the impression you are intended to receive is that Mr. Durant supports Mr. Welch's effort to show that history, especially that of the Greeks and Romans, demonstrates that democracy *is* "merely a deceptive phrase," and is *not* a republic.

When you look more closely, you discover first that no reference is given as to where Mr. Durant has written any of the quotations made from him in the pamphlet. Perhaps Mr. Welch is just careless; perhaps he was in a hurry; or perhaps he did not care to have us double-check on his quotation. What do you think?

Was Mr. Welch afraid, first of all, that we might find out that democracy as we in the United States know it, was *never tried* in Greece or Rome? So it is hard to know just what they could have "found out" about it. But the *Blue Book* confidently asserts:

> And democracy, of course, in government or organization, as the Greeks and Romans both found out . . . is merely a deceptive phrase . . . etc. (p. 159).

Oh yes, "of course." Except for one tiny flaw: *they never tried democracy as we have it.* And this Mr. Durant makes clear enough, in the book Mr. Welch does not care to name, entitled *The Life of Greece.* What was the famous Athenian "democracy" like? Turn to pages 254-57 of Mr. Durant and see. First, "only a small minority of the people can read." Second, there were only 43,000 citizens out of a population of 315,000—the rest were slaves, 115,000 of them; and aliens, 28,000 of them; and women and children, neither of whom had any political rights at all.

Yes, let us pay all honor to these pioneers of the human spirit, the Greeks. But let's not be dragging them in to "prove" to Americans that democracy is a "deceptive phrase." It was, indeed, "deceptive" for the Greek slaves who outnumbered their masters two to one or more; it was, indeed, a "fraud" for the "aliens" who had no way of getting citizenship; it was, indeed, "demagoguery" for the women, who simply did not count. In correcting all these defects, we would have far more to teach the Greeks about democracy than they would have to teach us. Mr. Welch's bold reference to "history" as proof that democracy is a "fraud" while republic is something quite different, falls, as usual, flat on his face.

True to form, Mr. Welch quietly neglects also to tell us that Mr. Durant speaks well of what Athens made of the "democracy" it did achieve. Durant says:

> Such is Athenian democracy—the narrowest and fullest in history. . . . The faults of the system will appear vividly as history unfolds. . . . But every government is imperfect . . . and perhaps only this chaotic democracy can release the energy that will lift Athens to one of the peaks of history. Never before or since has political life, within the circle of citizen-

ship, been so intense or creative . . . (*The Life of Greece*, p. 266).

So the Greeks can show us that "democracy" is a "fraud"? Will Durant does not think so. And although Mr. Welch carefully uses Durant's name, he just as carefully omits any reference to the quotation I have just given. If we are going to talk about the Greeks at all, then why not first say *honestly* that their form of democracy was not *like* ours, but was what Durant calls the "narrowest" in history; and why not, second, *honestly* admit that with all its faults, "democracy" did in Greece lift "Athens to one of the peaks of history." Why play games with history? And why try to fool the American people?

If you will study *Federalist Paper* No. 63, you will notice that our Founding Fathers knew all about Athenian "democracy," and they hoped to endow America with a form of that democracy which would be based upon all of the people instead of a limited few; and which would curb the "faction" to which Greek democracy was too often victim. The discussion of faction we have already seen in *Federalist* No. 10. Perhaps the JBS is, understandably, sensitive on the subject of "faction".

In his discussion of Rome, Mr. Welch again tries to make selective use of Will Durant. As usual, no volume is named and no page is mentioned, but it is now Mr. Durant's *Caesar and Christ,* and Mr. Welch's quotation comes from page 165. This is what Mr. Welch's pamphlet says:

> "Without checks and balances," Dr. Will Durant summarizes one statement of Cicero, "monarchy becomes despotism, aristocracy becomes oligarchy, democracy becomes mob rule, chaos, and dictatorship" (*Republics and Democracies*, p. 15).

Do I need to repeat it for anyone besides Mr. Welch and the JBS? Cicero is saying that democracy may exist *with* checks and balances, or *without* checks and balances. If it exists without them, it becomes "mob rule." But what if, like the American democracy, it exists *with* checks and balances? Cicero ought to say, if the JBS wants to use "history" to prove its argument about the difference between democracy and republic, then, I repeat, Cicero ought to say that democracy *with* checks and balances is a "republic." But this he does not say. And if, as the JBS asserts, the Romans "found out" that democracy is a "fraud," then Cicero should be saying that, too. But what does he say? Let us go back to Mr. Durant, and read this:

> Democracy is good when the people are virtuous, which, Cicero thought, is never (*Caesar and Christ,* p. 165).

And our Founding Fathers thought that Cicero was right about democracy—it is *good*—but wrong about "the people." For our Founding Fathers always turned to "the people" as virtuous enough to govern themselves. Jefferson spoke for the American spirit, accepting democracy but rejecting Cicero's pessimism, when he said in his First Inaugural Address:

> Sometimes it is said that man can not be trusted with the government of himself. Can he, then, be trusted with the government of others? Or have we found angels in the forms of kings to govern him? Let history answer this question (*Documents of American History,* p. 187).

Well, fellow American, where do you take your stand? With Cicero and the JBS? Or with Thomas Jefferson?

The argument from "history," like the argument from "etymology," falls on its face! The Greeks and Romans have *not* "found out" for us that democracy is a "fraud." And they do *not* say that democracy cannot exist in the form of a republic. On the contrary, Dr. Will Durant points out that the "narrow" democracy of Athens lifted the Greeks to heights of achievement; and Cicero calls "democracy" as good as the people are virtuous.

And this is the real challenge that the Greeks and Romans lay upon us today: can you, and can I, and can we all together, be virtuous enough, honest enough, and dedicated enough, to *make democracy work in our generation*? Dare we act on our own Declaration that "all men are created equal"? Ask a JBS member that question some time. And if he says, "Yes," ask him why, then, if all men are equal, is he in an organization that needs to take direction from "the top"?

There is the last JBS contention: that democracy is rule "of men" and republic is rule "of law."

Don't you see through that play on words? None of the dictionaries defines democracy or republic in this way. The *Federalist Papers* do not. The Greeks and Romans give such definition no support. All we have is the JBS determination to make this definition on their own.

Now, if men wish to fly in the face of the dictionary, of their own experience, of their greatest leaders, and of history itself, just to define words in their own way, let them go. No harm will come of it, and they can enjoy talking to themselves. But for those of us who want to *know,* ask yourself just one question: *Who makes law?*

If *republic* is government "of law," as the JBS says, then where does this "law" come from? Obviously, from *men*. And how is this law administered? Obviously, by *men*.

Then what happens to that pretended distinction between government "by law" and "by men"? *There is none,* and this is why all authorities on government do *not* define types of government by the distinction between "laws" and "men." If government is not "by law," then it is no longer government, but anarchy. And this is what the JBS is really trying to do: *treat democracy as if it were anarchy.*

Now, it is true that democracy *can become* anarchy. But then it is no longer democracy. Just keep the terms straight. Any other form of government can also become anarchy. But then it is no longer that other form of government. And when the JBS says that there is a drive on now to make our country a "democracy" (see Mr. Welch's pamphlet, pp. 24-34) they mean a drive to make our country into "anarchy." And every piece of legislation that the JBS does not like is said to point in that direction.

Which is a nice game if you can make it go. The JBS wants to have it both ways: on the one hand, it warns us all that the legislation of the last few decades is carefully planned to make us one of "four provinces in a world-wide Communist dominion ruled by police-state methods from the Kremlin." (*Blue Book,* p. 9). Sounds "shocking" enough, but what do you wager that any time now the JBS will quietly substitute "Peking" for "the Kremlin" just to send the "shock-score" up. But notice: "ruled by police-state methods. . . ." and in just "a few years," too.

On the other hand, the JBS keeps warning us that America is being pushed by the so-called "Liberals" and other villains from its heritage as a "republic" into becoming a "democracy." This is what Mr. Welch's whole pamphlet is designed to lead up to: America, he says, is fast becoming a "democracy" (p. 31). And by "democracy" the JBS means, of course, "mob rule" or "mobocracy." This will also come to pass in "a few years."

But a "mobocracy" is the exact *opposite* of "police-state" rule from the Kremlin, or Peking, or anywhere else. So America is moving rapidly, according to the JBS, in two exactly opposite directions at the same time! Just swallow whichever threat happens to "shock" you the more! All the JBS really asks is that you become confused enough to turn to a "boss" who will tell you exactly what to think, to say, and to do. For the "shock treatment" has very little to do with facts and truth, as we have seen by examining its methods; but it hopes to have much to do with spreading confusion, fear, and suspicion.

For the JBS will try to tell us that *first* will come "mobocracy," and *then* will come control from the top. Yes, this is exactly what the JBS wants to accomplish: first, create all the confusion, and all the illusion of "mobocracy" that the "shock treatment" can be used to produce; and, *then,* expect that Americans will surrender their own pattern of sovereignty from "the people" up, in exchange for the JBS pattern of "from the top" down.

But Americans don't buy your model, JBS. Our Founding Fathers rejected it. Our great patriots scorned it. The vast majority of their descendants, who stand proudly on their own two feet, see through your "shock treatment" just "as plain as day." And that is why the JBS goal of a "million members" is still a fanciful mirage, "shock" us as you will. Call democracy "that footstool of tyrants" (*B.B.,* fn. no. 14) all you like; you are still not going to stand on that footstool to tell Americans what to do.

Yes, we read on page 138 of the *Blue Book,* this:

> The true *americanist* [italics and small "a" in the B.B.] believes that the individual should retain the freedom to make his own bargain with life, and the responsibility for the results of that bargain.

Moreover, we observe JBS recognition of the right of conscience, as footnote no. 27 puts it:

> Our members are told specifically and emphatically in our bulletins, about once every three months, never to carry out any of our requests or to do anything for the Society that is against their individual consciences or even contrary to their best judgment. If they find themselves too constantly and continuously in disagreement with our activities, then probably they do not belong in the Society and may wish to resign.

But if an "americanist" does "retain the freedom to make his own bargain with life," should that kind of American need to be "specifically and emphatically" *told* not to violate his conscience? And does he have to be re-told this elementary responsibility of "freedom" about once or twice *every three months*? Is the JBS so used to being bossed from the top, that it has to be "told" about that ultimate freedom, liberty of conscience, almost once a month?

And about this "freedom to make his own bargain with life," pause for a moment to see how the JBS practices what it preaches in this important matter. The source is the *Blue Book,* p. 85.

The year before the JBS was born, United Airlines decided to put on its planes the seal of the United Nations, and to print under it the words "We Believe." United Airlines was thus exercising its right to make its own bargain with life. This is what the *Blue Book* has just told us it stands for.

What happened? A number of anti-U.N. groups initiated what the *Blue Book* calls a "spontaneous letter-writing campaign" designed to "force" United Airlines to remove the U.N. insigne. Letter writing, of course, is also an American freedom. And the expression to United Airlines of approval or of disapproval is a public right. But a "letter-writing campaign" to "force" someone else to make "your" bargain with life, instead of "his own" bargain with life, can hardly be "americanist." Not, at least, as the *Blue Book* defines "americanist." Listen once more to what it says:

> The true americanist believes that the individual
> should retain the freedom to make his own bargain
> with life ... (p. 138).

Obviously, therefore, the *Blue Book* should denounce this wholly un-americanist "campaign" designed to "force" United Airlines to abide, not by its "own" but by other Americans' judgment of the U.N. Let United Airlines make its own bargain with life; and let each other American, individual or corporation, make its own. This is what the JBS pretends to stand for.

But what, in fact, comes of this talk of "freedom" when the chips are down? You can guess. The *Blue Book* brags of the success of that "campaign" against United Airlines. Listen: the campaign was "able to force United Airlines to back down completely and publicly admit that they had made a mistake."

Judging from its practice, rather than from its propaganda, the JBS means by "freedom" the right of everyone to make, not "his own" but the JBS "bargain with life." In fact, the *Blue Book* brags that the letter-writing "campaign" forced United Airlines to back down against its "determined and entrenched opposition." All of a sudden, the "freedom" to make your own bargain with life becomes, if the JBS does not agree with you, a "determined and entrenched opposition."

Several years after this incident, the JBS undertook to dictate to the Xerox Corporation that *it* make, not its *own,* but the JBS bargain with life, and cancel a series of television programs which Xerox had announced. This corporation did *not* back down." And the JBS *Bulletin* screamed once and again *not* to support Xerox in its "americanist" right to choose its own mode of advertising. Oh no. That would be to practice what the Society preaches. Instead, the *Bulletin* screamed for more letters, and more letters, demanding that Xerox take the television series off the air.

Says the *Blue Book*:

> We would institute the organized planning and control to make full and effectively coordinated use of the powerful letter-writing weapon that lies so ready at hand (p. 84).

Yes, and "we" will tell our loyal members exactly

which of their fellow citizens must be "forced" if possible to make the JBS "bargain with life" instead of their "own." If this is "americanist," then we had better be just plain *American*. Americans don't have, and don't want, a "boss" who shouts, "Come on, Boy! Let's get those letters out! You write 'em this way. . . !"

"The true americanist believes that the individual should retain the freedom to make his own bargain with life. . ."

Well, well. Perhaps the JBS isn't truly "americanist"?

Yes, let's ask that question, in conclusion. If the JBS is not formed on an American "model," and it surely is not, then on what model is it patterned? The *Blue Book* does not ask, or answer, that embarrassing question. There are, however, some hints. Read them and judge for yourself what model the *Blue Book* looks to as its teacher:

1—One of the greatest weaknesses and mistakes on the conservative side has been that almost all of the organizations, real ones or just letter-head outfits, have been put together for *general* purposes. The Communists have been far smarter (pp. 86-87).

2—The front business, like a lot of techniques the Communists use, can be made to cut both ways (p. 90).

3—It isn't numbers we have to worry about in this connection, but the courage on the part of our followers to stick their necks out and play rough—the same as the Communists do all the time (p. 91).

4—But the possible use of petitions is fairly obvious. Goodness knows the Communists have proved their subtle value and effectiveness (p. 94).

5—This question technique, when skillfully used in this way, is mean and dirty. But the Communists we are after are meaner and dirtier . . . (p. 96).

6—The John Birch Society is to be a monolithic body. The Catholic Church is a body. . . . The Communist Party is a body (pp. 158; 109).

7—If I had sufficient resources available and sufficiently accepted authority over one million dedicated supporters . . . so that I could coordinate the activities of those million men and women with some degree of positiveness and efficiency approaching the coordination by the Communists of their members and fellow travelers . . . here are some of the things I would do (pp. 76-77).

8—We would institute the organized planning and control to make full and effectively coordinated use of the powerful letter-writing weapon that lies so ready to hand. The Communists boast that they can now land 50,000 individually written letters in Washington . . . (p. 84).

9—Letter writing, of a different order of planned continuity and volume than anything attempted before—except on a somewhat more sporadic scale by the Communists themselves . . . (p. 86).

10—Communism . . . there has been brilliant control and coordination, by central authority. . . . The John Birch Society will operate under completely authoritative control at all levels (pp. 72, 159).

11—. . . we should like to call to their [critics'] attention *one* difference between the Communists and ourselves. You join the Communist Party, and you are told what to do. You refuse to do it enough times, and you are shot in some dark alley or pushed off a subway platform in front of a moving train. You join the Birch Society, and you are asked to do certain things, *if you agree.* You refuse to do them enough times—and we give you your money back (fn. 15).

That is *one* significant difference. You, fellow American, decide for yourself what the "score" here is. What model does the JBS take as its teacher, as it tries to teach us what good Americanism, or at least what a good "americanist" is?

We know it rejects the American model of an adopted constitution, the election of officers, and control from the membership up. The *Blue Book* half suspects what your conclusion will be, and says:

> For we need disciplined pullers at the oars, and not passengers in the boat. Now that last statement may put you in mind of the Communist principle of "the dedicated few" as enunciated by Lenin. And we are, in fact, willing to draw on all successful human experience in organizational matters, so long as it does not involve any sacrifice of morality in the means used to achieve an end (*B.B.*, p. 166).

This is blunt enough. And clearly separates, once more, the JBS from the American tradition. For our forefathers were absolutely *un*-willing "to draw on all successful human experience" with government from "the top." Successful or not, tyranny was anathema to